Shaolin
Five Animals

少林五形拳

Shaolin
Five Animals

By Doc-Fai Wong and Jane Hallander

UP

DISCLAIMER

Although both Unique Publications and the author(s) of this martial arts book have taken great care to ensure the authenticity of the information and techniques contained herein, we are not responsible, in whole or in part, for any injury which may occur to the reader or readers by reading and/or following the instructions in this publication. We also do not guarantee that the techniques and illustrations described in this book will be safe and effective in a self-defense or training situation. It is understood that there exists a potential for injury when using or demonstrating the techniques herein described. It is essential that before following any of the activities, physical or otherwise, herein described, the reader or readers first should consult his or her physician for advice on whether practicing or using the techniques described in this publication could cause injury, physical or otherwise. Since the physical activities described herein could be too sophisticated in nature for the reader or readers, it is essential a physician be consulted. Also, federal, state or local laws may prohibit the use or possession of weapons described herein. A thorough examination must be made of the federal, state and local laws before the reader or readers attempts to use these weapons in a self-defense situation or otherwise. Neither Unique Publications nor the author(s) of this martial arts book guarantees the legality or the appropriateness of the techniques or weapons herein contained.

ISBN: 0-86568-080-9
Library of Congress Catalog Card Number: 86-50441

Designer: Danilo Silverio
Editors: Dave Cater and Sandra Segal

 UNIQUE
PUBLICATIONS
4201 Vanowen Place
Burbank, CA 91505

Table
of Contents

Preface

To standardize the Chinese terminology in this book, *pinyin* romanization was chosen. Pinyin is the romanization used in Mainland China, and is rapidly being adopted as the romanization of choice for many non-Chinese publications. Since it is the romanization seen most often in present-day publications, we have decided to follow suit and standardize this book to pinyin.

Certain terms are best known by their Yale or Wade-Giles romanizations. Those are listed in parenthesis immediately following the pinyin romanization.

Others, like the term kung-fu, are so well-known in their present state, we leave them in whatever romanization they are best known.

少林五形拳歷史

Chapter One

History of Shaolin Five Animals

Chinese martial arts are unique in the emphasis placed on the study of animal habits and fighting tactics. Throughout the centuries, the nature of birds, snakes, land animals and insects have been faithfully imitated to recreate the particular individual essence that makes each an efficient fighter.

These creatures were studied not only for their fighting abilities, but also for any health benefits they could contribute to their human counterparts.

There was no single source of study of animal forms in China. As martial artists saw an opportunity to improve or change their kung-fu systems, they quickly injected the techniques and spirit of the animal that inspired the change. Some styles were even given the name of the animal after which they were patterned: praying mantis and white crane, for instance.

One animal study that had an enormous impact on Chinese martial arts was the *Shaolin five animals*, an integral part of the Shaolin martial arts system, and a strong influence in the development of other kung-fu styles.

Chan (Zen) Buddhism became established in China during the Nan Bei Chao (North-South dynasty) about A.D. 550. The Indian monk, Bodhidharma (known as *Da-Mo* in Chinese), who was to become the first patriarch of Chan Buddhism in China, traveled until he reached Songshan mountain in Henan province, the site of the Shaolin Temple. Bodhidharma spent the next nine years in meditation. Then at the advanced age of 76, he began teaching health arts to the monks of the Shaolin Temple. Bodhidharma was not the founder of either the Shaolin Temple or its martial arts system; he simply lived in the temple and taught the monks. During his years of residence at the Shaolin Temple, Bodhidharma noticed that monks who practiced many hours of meditation each day were in poor physical condition. They couldn't perform the physical labors necessary to maintain the monastery, and if attacked by bandits, could not even defend the Shaolin Temple. Therefore, he taught exercises designed to both promote health and strength, and give the monks some basic self-defense techniques.

Bodhidharma gave the Shaolin monks three sets of exercises: *Lohan shi ba shou* (18 hands of Arhats), *yi jin jing* (book of changing tendons), and *xi shui jing* (book of washing bone marrow). These exercises influenced Chinese martial arts so much, Bodhidharma is often referred to as the "father of kung-fu."

Before Bodhidharma came to China, martial arts were militaristic in nature. Only nobility and professional soldiers were allowed to openly study fighting arts. Spears and swords were the most common weapons, and training in their use was reserved for the military. If the public was taught, it was on a limited scale.

The Tang dynasty (A.D. 618-907) was a warring period in China's history. Martial arts and the development of more personalized specialty weapons flourished during this era. Shaolin Temple monks, at the request of the Tang government, used their martial training to help fight threats to the Tang rulers. From that time, the rest of China knew that some Shaolin monks had been martial artists before joining the Shaolin Temple and their new duties were to protect its occupants and land. Martial art training within the Shaolin Temple had served to expand and polish their fighting backgrounds.

The period following the Tang dynasty was one of creative expansion for China's martial arts. Song Tai Zu (Zhao Kuangyin), the first emperor of the Song dynasty (A.D. 960-976), was a martial artist, famous for his expertise with the three-sectioned staff. Song Tai Zu originated the *tai zu chang quan* (chang chuan) or long fist martial arts system.

A popular style today, *long fist* is considered by many to be the "grandfather" system of present-day kung-fu styles.

In the Southern Song dynasty, a famous general named Yue Fei made Chinese martial arts history with his spear techniques. However, more important than Yue Fei's spear expertise was that he converted those same techniques, called *yue san shou*, into empty-hand techniques. Other martial artists took those hand techniques and developed them into *mind and intention boxing*, known as *xing-I* (hsing-I). This was then the beginning of the soft or *internal* Chinese martial art styles.

Martial arts gained excellence during the Ming dynasty (A.D. 1368-1644). During this period, a Taoist priest, Zhang San Feng, noticed those practicing martial arts used only brutal, tense force to deliver blows. They overexerted themselves, sweated profusely, and were breathless after even a simple workout. Zhang San Feng believed this was contrary to Taoist and good health principles. Therefore, he combined exercises for health and martial arts into a soft flowing exercise designed to develop internal organs and condition bones and muscles. Natural relaxation was the guiding principle behind Zhang's system. He believed both internal and external training could be effectively combined into one complete martial art. His emphasis was on soft strength for defensive purposes and hard striking fists to be used offensively. This theory led to the development of the soft Chinese martial art called *tai ji quan* (tai chi chuan).

Among the most important principles to come from Zhang San Feng's teaching is to attack when the opponent's "old" or original strength is exhausted, but before he has a chance to generate "new" strength. This theory has prevailed within kung-fu's soft internal systems, and has drastically changed Chinese martial arts.

Soon after, Chinese martial arts broke into hard and soft styles. The Shaolin system was known as a hard external system; since internal styles instantly became popular, the Shaolin system almost became extinct.

At the end of the Ming dynasty (A.D. 1368-1644), a practitioner-turned-Shaolin-monk named Zhue Yuen changed the course of Shaolin martial arts. Zhue Yuen had been an expert in empty-hand fighting and sword techniques before he became a Buddhist monk. When he joined the Shaolin Temple he realized Shaolin kung-fu was too external and employed too much force against force. Zhue Yuen redesigned the Shaolin system to fit a more balanced structure of external and internal strengths. He traveled throughout China incorporating unusual, but still practiced martial arts, into his new Shaolin system.

When Zhue Yuen arrived at the town of Lan Zhou he met a martial artist named Li Sou, who introduced him to Bai Yu Feng, another famous martial artist.

The three eventually returned to the Shaolin Temple and founded the five animal form (*wu xing quan*). This completed the *new* Shaolin system.

The Shaolin system originally was comprised of 18 exercises or techniques. Bai Yu Feng increased the original 18 to 128 movements. Those 128 movements then were divided into five separate animal imitations.

Each of the animals — tiger, leopard, crane, snake and dragon — have different outstanding and distinctive features.

According to Bai Yu Feng, all people must develop five aspects of their being to condition the entire body. They are: physical strength, bone development, libido, chi development, and internal spirit. The first two are external and the last three are internal training. Bai Yu Feng also believed when all five are combined, the result is a far superior martial artist. The Shaolin five animal form was devised to assist in the development of all five strengths.

龍

Chapter Two

Dragon (Long Xing)

The Chinese dragon is no relation to the Western world's fire-breathing dragon or to any prehistoric dinosaurlike beast. It is strictly a product of spiritual beliefs and is listed in Buddhist text as a supernatural animal that can appear or disappear at will, and make itself any size.

According to Buddhist writings, dragons live in oceans. Since dragons live in large bodies of water, their association with the rest of the world is through water. If a dragon wishes to become visible, anyone can see him. If not, then only those who have reached a high level of enlightenment can view this special animal. The Chinese also believe dragons produce rain, and when they do decide to make themselves visible, they're seen on clouds.

Chinese dragons have snakelike bodies covered with scales. They also have lizardlike arms and legs which end in sharp claws. The head resembles a serpent's. Since Shaolin martial arts are derived from Buddhist origins, the dragon was a perfect candidate to represent one of the five animals.

As with its mythical namesake, Shaolin dragon-style fighting transcends the easily understood *real* world of external martial arts and enters the *spiritual* world of internal strength and power.

The dragon represents internal strength, although it does have some external training benefits. Since dragons are not actual living beasts, many dragon techniques are variations of the characteristics of other kung-fu animals. For instance, dragon movements are soft and circular, similar to, but not exactly like, those of the snake.

However, dragon techniques should not be confused with those of the Shaolin snake. Although both are lizardlike, the snake has no legs, while the dragon's claws form an important element of its fighting style.

While Shaolin snake techniques contain more soft coiling actions and fingertip strikes, dragon techniques are represented by soft circular movements that terminate with hard *sudden* power. Therefore, the snake exhibits only soft power, while the dragon uses a force that represents a combination of both hard and soft training.

Since Chinese dragons have claws, the Shaolin dragon form possesses a claw-hand technique that is sometimes confused with the tiger claw version. However, the dragon claw hand (*long zhua*) is a grab, while a tiger claw (*hu zhua*) is a squeezing, tearing motion. Also, unlike the tiger variety, dragon claws are not downward ripping techniques. Instead they are softer, more circular, and primarily locking or pulling techniques.

The primary hand technique displayed in the dragon form is the claw (*long zhua*). Not all dragon hand movements are claw hands. There also are palm and fist

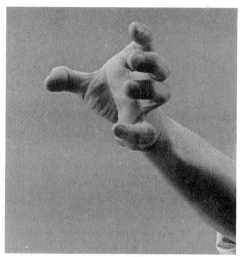

attacks. However, the claw is the most often used hand technique. Dragon claws are characteristically flat claw hands designed for grabbing arms, ears, and other extremities.

Shaolin's dragon style is famous for several different claw-hand techniques:

1) *Shen long xian zhua* (dragon swings his claw) is a sideways, horizontal swinging claw hand to the opposition's ribs, using the waist to generate power.

2) *Jin long shi zhua* (golden dragon tests his claws) is a jointlock delivered with both claw hands. The dragon practitioner uses his elbow to bring pressure against his adversary's arm. If necessary, he can break it.

3) *Shen long xia hai* (dragon sinks into the ocean) starts out as a grab with both claw hands. The dragon stylist then sinks his weight, pulling his adversary off balance and onto the floor.

Although the claw hand is the most often seen dragon technique, the form also contains fist and palm strikes. Some of the dragon fists are:

1) *Wu long bai wei* (dragon swings his tail) is similar to a spinning backfist. The

dragon practitioner uses his waist with a whiplike action to obtain power.

2) *Qing long chu hai* (green dragon comes up from the ocean) is a rotating fist strike. One hand pulls the opponent forward as the other fist strikes.

3) *Jin long wang ri* (golden dragon looks at the sun) is a forward uppercut fist with the dragon stylist's free hand blocking over his head.

The Shaolin dragon form also contains palm strikes similar to the striking motion of its sister, the snake form. The difference is that the dragon strike is a claw strike, not a fingertip attack as with the snake.

In the days of the Shaolin Temple, dragon claw training involved special hand and arm strengthening exercises, called *long zhua gong*. Five animal students would slowly lift and hold heavy clay jars. They started with empty jars and as their strength increased, added water until the jars were full. Then they repeated the procedure with sand and finally rocks of increasing size and weight.

The actual dragon movements also encourage the student to use his waist to generate power, rather than merely his shoulders and arms. This useful training habit comes from an imitation of the whiplike action of a dragon's long tail.

The dragon form's primary contribution to Shaolin five animal training is its internal conditioning and training, which comes in the form of *qi* (chi or ki) development. *Qi* is the body's internally generated energy and power. When qi is properly developed, it can be combined with external strength to produce devastating results. For instance, the external dragon claw is itself powerful and strong, but still limited by actual physical strength. When the five animal practitioner puts his qi into his dragon claw hand, he generates power many times that of the external strike alone.

Several methods of developing qi can be utilized in the dragon form. Breathing correctly is one important method. Breathing should be relaxed, using the lower body to pull in air, rather than just the chest muscles. Correct internal breathing in the dragon form is not a tense dynamic breathing, but instead is soft and relaxed. When done properly, it will help pull the qi down lower into the *dan tian* area, the location of the body's internal energy and strength. Correct breathing techniques also help to fill the student's body with circulating qi, which makes the body more flexible and relaxed.

9

The actual fighting application of the dragon form breathing techniques is a type of *hard and soft* breathing, sometimes referred to as *soft carries hard*. The five animal practitioner's breathing is soft and relaxed until the strike is made, when it becomes a sharp expulsion of breath and power upon contact.

While training in the Shaolin dragon form, the student should be soft and slow to develop his qi, as if he were practicing tai ji quan (tai chi chuan). If he is too tense, his qi will not flow. He should emit hard external power only upon contact with an object. As there is no contact involved with forms practice, he must concentrate only upon the development of his qi to give him the internal strength needed for any contact he might come across.

Since the Chinese dragon is a spiritually powerful animal, the Shaolin five animal student should picture himself the same way. If he feels himself to be a dragonlike fighter, he can utilize and take advantage of certain dragon characteristics. For instance, dragons can appear and disappear. Although the martial artist can't physically disappear, he can use dragon *spirit* to fool his opponent into thinking he's attacking from one direction when in reality his attack suddenly appears from the opposite direction.

He also can put the dragon's ability to expand or shrink into practice. The dragon practitioner can become large to his opposition by using his body as a weapon. Or, he can use only his fingertips to produce damage to a small area of his enemy's body.

Dragons are reputed to move from ocean to clouds, as does the dragon student. Dragon techniques include both takedowns (oceans) and throws (clouds).

Part of the dragon's spirit is his *intention*. This type of qi development is called *shen*. It allows the five animal practitioner to focus his qi out through his eyes to produce a special kind of spirit or intention. Often, eye contact is enough to scare away the enemy. People who are ill cannot produce shen, which is a byproduct only of those with healthy bodies and well-developed qi.

The Shaolin dragon form gives the student a vehicle with which to combine his internal energy with his external strengths to produce awesome power.

虎

Chapter Three

Tiger
(Hu Xing)

An old Chinese saying states, "One mountain has no room for two tigers." In China, tigers are considered so fierce that only one can live in peace on a mountain. Since there are no lions in China, tigers are called the *king* of all land beasts.

The same is true for the tiger form in the Shaolin five animal set. Shaolin monks watched tigers in action. They observed their strength, courage, and power, and decided the animal had an immense value to their kung-fu. Thus, the five animal form reflects a strong influence of the tiger in action.

The tiger form differs from the other four animals in that its training is designed to produce strong bone. A tiger is a fast animal with a strong attack. His attack is a pressing action, like being run down by an automobile. A tiger's strength is a hard, forceful, external strength.

The tiger form not only develops power, but also conditions the necessary tendons and bones to harden and strengthen the spine and neck. To exude hard external power, the neck and back must become tense and strong. The tiger form provides that ability.

Since much of kung-fu's power comes from strong stances and powerful waist action, the martial artist must have a well-conditioned back. The tiger form develops a strong, sturdy back.

The primary technique used in the tiger form is a *hu zhua* (tiger claw). The tiger claw hand is formed by curling the fingers and thumb into a *claw* position. It is a short, straight strike with pulls, twists, tears, or presses upon impact. Targets for a hu zhua are face, neck, groin, arms or wrists. At impact, the hu zhua palm is pressed hard against the opposition to give the five animal practitioner's fingers more gripping material. Then he either can pull straight down or twist with his claw hand.

The tiger claw hand differs from a dragon claw in that where the dragon claw is a squeezing locking technique, hu zhua is an explosive ripping or pressing action.

Although most tiger form techniques develop around the tiger claw, there is a technique known as *lao hu tai tou* (tiger raises his head), which is represented by a fist instead of a palm strike. Since a tiger can use his head to strike, la hu tai tou utilizes a regular closed fist to imitate the big cat's head.

Besides lao hu tai tou, other distinctive and colorfully named tiger strikes include: *meng hu hui tou* (wild tiger looks back), which employs a cross-stance in conjunction with a hu zhua, and *er hu qin yang* (hungry tiger catches a lamb), a straight tiger claw which ends in a trapping and pressing motion.

Another tiger technique important to Shaolin's five animals is called *lao hu dian tou* (tiger nods his head). One application of this technique is where one hand grabs the opponent's wrist with a tiger claw, while the other fist strikes straight down. The other application of lao hu dian tou is a jointlock where one hand countergrabs a grabbed wrist and twists the opponent's arm. At the same time, the other fist presses down on a pressure point located behind and above the elbow. This brings sudden pain.

Shaolin tiger techniques do include palm strikes, such as *meng hu tui shan* (tiger pushes the mountain). One hand grabs the attacker's punching fist with a hu zhua, while the other hand simultaneously thrusts into the rib area, using the palm portion of a tiger claw hand.

There are also special kicking techniques that represent the tiger in Shaolin five animals. One kick is called *hu wei tui* or *tiger tail kick* and is known in the Shaolin five animals form as *lazy tiger stretches his back leg*. It is a back kick, performed

with the five animal practitioner's body parallel to the ground, and his arms outstretched in front.

When using the tiger claw, the whole hand is important, not just the fingers. Therefore, it is key for the student to develop his fingers, palms and legs.

To condition his fingers for hu zhua, the tiger stylist throws small heavy sandbags into the air and catches them with his fingertips. He also works with a sandbag, where he can practice hu zhua grabs at full speed.

In ancient China, five animal practitioners strengthened their fingers and arms by lifting clay jars filled at different levels with gravel. This is similar to the training of the dragon form.

In the old days, five animal students grabbed and squeezed tree branches to condition and develop strength in their fingers, hands, and arms for their hu zhuas. Nowadays, the modern martial artist squeezes a rubber ball to attain the same effect.

Since he uses his whole hand to deliver an effective hu zhua, the five animal student develops his arms and fingers by practicing push-ups on his fingers instead of his hands. To condition his back and neck, he practices a special type of push-up, designed to build strength in his arms, back, and legs. This push-up requires the kung-fu student to pull his body forward until his chest almost touches the floor. Then he reverses the action and pulls back his body, using his back muscles. With this push-up, the motion is similar to rolling forward and then back, rather than straight up and down, as with regular push-ups.

There is much more to the tiger form than its tiger claw hand. There are special breathing techniques that help develop power and force. When the student practices, he emits certain breathing sounds at specified times during the form. These breathing sounds are an important training feature. They build the tiger stylist's stamina by forcing him to expel carbon dioxide and replacing it with the oxygen necessary to deliver power with his tiger strikes. Yelling out the breathing sounds also keeps the martial artist's spirit high, an important factor when moving with the speed and force required in the tiger form. He expels his breath and emits a *wak* sound with every hu zhua in the form.

Another important segment of the Shaolin tiger form is *spirit*. When the martial student performs the tiger portions of five animals, he should have a tense neck and angry eyes, as does a tiger when he fights. He must think and feel as if he were a wild tiger coming down from a mountain. Power comes often from fierceness. When the five animal student makes his spirit the same as that of a wild tiger, he adds extra power to his strikes. He also becomes less vulnerable to any enemy attack, since his fierce tiger spirit prevails.

蛇

Chapter Four

Snake (She Xing)

The snake seems like an unlikely animal to see in the Shaolin five animal form, since it lacks legs for rapid movement and by nature is sly and soft, rather than aggressive and powerful. However, those are exactly the reasons why the snake was included in the Shaolin system.

The purpose of the snake form is to develop and cultivate the internal energy called *qi*. Qi is the essence that gives the five animal practitioner focus and penetrating power far superior to ordinary external strikes.

Since the snake has no arms or legs, the reptile must move with a zigzagging twisting action of his body. To be an effective fighter, the snake must do something to compensate for his lack of limbs: first, the snake can coil his body and raise straight up, as does a cobra, into a striking position. From that coiled position, with devastating speed and accuracy, he straightens his body in a strike toward his prey. The snake gains a great power and force from just the momentum and twisting action of his *coiled* strike.

The other advantage, and perhaps even more important than the snake's unique striking technique, is in developing and releasing internal energy (qi) with every strike. Since he is a calm, relaxed animal, the snake possesses much more qi than other animals. Therefore, when he combines his internal energy with his external

striking technique, the snake becomes a formidable and powerful adversary.

The snake form differs from the other five animal forms in that, through its relaxed floating movements, it delivers a power that is both hard and soft. Most other animal styles utilize a tense, aggressive force to strike down their adversaries. There are no fists to be seen in the snake form. The strikes are all penetrating palm and fingertip attacks.

The tiger, for instance, is the opposite of the snake. Its strength is strictly external. Tiger stylists are noisy and active, even going so far as to make loud external sounds with each strike to gain extra force. The snake's energy is quiet and internal. The snake makes no sound as it administers a soft, penetrating blow.

Also, all snake techniques are of the advanced martial level where blocks and strikes are made simultaneously. There is no difference between offense and defense, since defense instantly becomes offense and vice versa. Coiled or circular snake techniques often have defensive beginnings that change into straight offensive strikes, making the speed of attack not as vital as *smoothness* to the snake stylist.

There are several types of fingertip strikes seen in the Shaolin snake form. One strike recreates the tongue of the snake by extending the index and middle finger while simultaneously folding back the other fingers. This strike is called *bai she tu xin* (white snake throws out his tongue) and is usually targeted toward soft vital areas, such as the eyes.

Another fingertip technique called *qing she chu dong* (snake comes out of his hole) places the fingers together to form a fingertip attack that resembles a coiled cobra's head. The snake stylist's fingers lash out from a bent elbow to cumulate in an extended arm in much the same manner that a cobra would strike at his prey. This strike can also be employed as an upper block that will easily convert into a deadly blow to the throat or eyes.

Shui she shang an (water snake swims to the surface) is an uppercut fingertip strike directed at the pressure point located at the armpit or throat.

Besides initiating fighting techniques, animal forms usually resemble the attitude and spirit of that particular animal. Since an animal's fighting habits are based upon his instinctive nature, it is important to preserve that nature in the martial art form. Therefore, it is essential when practicing the snake form, the five animal student keep his whole body alive and moving. Since this form uses both soft and hard power, it is necessary to administer soft, circular force from the arms, and harder, external power from the hands at the moment of contact.

The most important contribution of the snake form is the development of qi, which is obtained through relaxation and concentration. When training in the snake form, the student should practice being calm and soft. He will imitate the long body that is generating energy with every movement. To help relax the five animal student, all snake portions of the form should be practiced slowly and with concentration. If it is practiced in this manner, each part of his body will be relaxed and connected. Relaxation contributes to a soft, flexible body. Concentration leads to calmness and clear thinking, necessary attributes for any martial artist.

By practicing the snake form, the five animal student will learn to put his qi energy through his arm and out to his fingertips. When he isn't touching his opponent, there appears to be no strength. However, when contact is made, strength is instantly produced.

There is no external fingertip strengthening and development involved with the snake form. The five animal student's fingers will have been conditioned by the special exercises used in connection with tiger, dragon, and crane forms.

It is important the student practice his snake form calmly and quietly, since that will develop his sensation and feeling for his opponent's next move. Actual contact made by the snake practitioner's arms has a similar *sticking* effect as does wing chun's sticky hands and tai ji quan's (tai chi chuan) push hands. When he isn't touching his opponent, there appears to be no strength at all, which doesn't mean that snake strikes are merely limp, soft touches that have a magical sting when they connect with a foe. Although the form looks soft in an actual fighting situation, the snake practitioner's actions are quick and forceful. Upon contact, the force of his internal energy creates a strength said to be over seven times an individual's normal power.

The snake has a special spirit. The five animal practitioner must be calm enough to mentally look inside his body and feel peaceful and quiet. Nothing will bother him externally.

If he develops the proper snake spirit, the five animal student will feel the energy flow from his spine through his arms and out his fingertips. As with a snake, the snake form stylist should move slowly (at the speed of a tai ji quan form) and deliberately before his strike or block is made. In actual use, many snake strikes are directed to the opponent's sensitive pressure points. These pressure points are vital areas of the body, that, when stimulated, can cause excessive pain, unconsciousness, or even death.

After assimilating Shaolin snake techniques, the five animal practitioner strikes with lightning speed and penetrating focus or intention.

鶴

Chapter Five

Crane
(He Xing)

The crane is only a bird, and yet he is a bird with a reputation for longevity and an extraordinary libido. Since such an excess of libido denotes an abundance of energy within the body, and since the crane also represents longevity, he was chosen to be one of the Shaolin five animals.

It is believed the crane lives a long life because his body contains a great amount of *jing*. *Jing* is the Chinese word for *essential energy*, but also translates to libido. The crane develops his jing easily, since he is a calm, quiet animal whose powers of concentration are not easily broken. An example of the crane's patience and concentration is his ability to stand for hours on just one leg, without shifting his weight.

Training in the Shaolin crane form was designed to help the martial artist hold his inside energy and consequently increase his strength, both internally and externally. It helps to develop his qi internally and, at the same time, hardens bone and muscle.

The crane has the same calm, quiet nature as the snake. And as with the snake, all crane movements are useful for overthrowing and controlling the opponent easily and with a minimum effort.

All crane form techniques are circular movements. They are always soft and relaxed. However, they still explode with quick, sudden power upon contact with the target. There are both long- and short-hand techniques. The short-hand move-

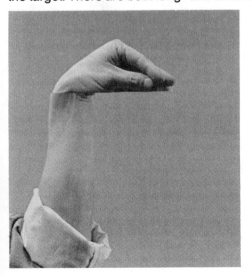

ments are often jointlocking techniques designed to disable the opponent's limbs, while the long, reaching techniques are often direct strikes to pressure points or other vital areas of the opponent's body.

The crane form is best known for its long outstretched winglike strikes, such as *he yi* (crane wing), a long-arm, circular, sweeping technique prevalent throughout Shaolin five animals. With the he yi technique, the arm down to and including the fingertips is the striking weapon. He yi represents the action of a crane spreading and opening his wings. This strike delivers a great amount of force, since the five animal stylist uses his full body power to generate energy. *Ye he kai yi* (crane strikes with his wing) is a crane wing technique intended to slice across the opponent's eyes.

The crane has a long neck, and uses it for long, stretched-out movements. Within the Shaolin five animal form, these are movements that usually terminate with a strike by his beak. The crane beak (*he zui*) is the most common symbol of the crane style of fighting. He zui is formed by closing fingers and thumb together to form a point, while still maintaining a slight bend in the wrist. Targets for a crane beak are the enemy's eyes, throat, and other vulnerable body areas.

A crane beak technique found in the five animal form is *shuang he tai tou* (twin cranes raise their heads). This is a crane beak performed in opposite directions by both hands and aimed at two opponents' solar plexuses.

The inside of a crane beak hand can also become a hooking hand, called *he jing* (crane neck), and used to first pull the opponent off balance and then to grab his neck, arms, or legs. Again, this strike is administered with soft, relaxed force. However, speed and a snapping action of the wrist adds concentrated power to the blow. *Bai he shou chao* (crane guards his nest) is a technique representing the use of a crane neck block.

Although the crane's beak is the best known representative of the crane form, an equally useful strike is called *he ding* (crane head). With this technique, the top of the crane practitioner's wrist imitates a crane's head. Just as a fighting crane might strike with the top of his head and follow with a thrust or push with his neck, the crane practitioner strikes with the top of his bent wrist and follows with a strong push into his opponent's already injured body. Many times, target areas for such a blow are the opposition's solar plexus, jaw or armpit. Not only does the crane stylist

launch an attack with the hard portion of his wrist, but he further pursues the attack by thrusting his bent wrist into the injured area, using his whole arm as the crane's neck.

Ye he shou dong (crane guards the cave) is a crane head technique that serves simultaneously as both a defensive and offensive action. The crane stylist blocks upward against an attacker's punching arm with his crane head wrist, striking a pressure point on the upper arm. This block carries so much power that it simultaneously becomes an offensive strike, leaving the opponent's arm painfully disabled.

There is also distinctive crane footwork seen in the Shaolin five animal form. *Bai he du li* (white crane stands on one leg) is a position in which the crane stylist stands on one leg with the other raised to avoid an oncoming low kick.

Immediately after dispersing his opponent's kick, the crane practitioner kicks with his already raised leg. The kick is called *bai he tan zhua* (crane stretches his claw) and is a front kick.

The crane is useful training for stretching and strengthening arms and fingers. Practicing the crane form also improves the martial artist's balance and speed, since the movements are quick and active, utilizing a loose, supple waist with light balanced footwork.

There are several special training techniques employed to condition and strengthen the crane practitioner's hands. Since this form relies upon concentrating the striking force into a small target area, it becomes important that the crane practitioner have strong, well-conditioned fingertips.

Besides practicing the special crane form exercises, the crane practitioner draws upon training from other animals to help strengthen his fingers. From the snake, he has learned to direct his qi into his fingertips. Dragon and tiger claw hands have already added external strength to his hands and fingers.

To develop his crane beak, the crane stylist will poke at firm sandbags. When his hand is well-conditioned from the bag, he switches from sandbags to plunging his crane beak fist into a bucket of coarse gravel. This training toughens his fingertips, making them into effective weapons when aimed at the right targets.

To condition his wrists for *he ding* (crane top), the crane stylist practices crane top blows against a sandbag and performs push-ups on his bent wrists.

Since he needs strong ankles to ensure proper balance when he performs *white crane stands on one leg*, the Shaolin crane form practitioner often works out wearing ankle weights.

The spirit of a crane is one of deep, relaxed concentration which encourages development of focus and intent within the Shaolin crane student.

豹

Chapter Six

Leopard (Bao Xing)

In China, the leopard or panther is second only to the tiger in terms of ferocity and power. Although smaller than a tiger, the leopard is actually stronger, for his size, and faster than the large, powerful tiger.

Tigers rely upon their size and the explosive force delivered by their short, thick muscle mass to overpower their adversaries. The leopard, on the other hand, is an animal comprised of long, smooth, even-toned muscle, enclosed within a sleek, fast body frame. Leopards depend upon lightning-fast speed and footwork to produce their strength and power.

Leopards do emit a solid power. However, it's not a tense, forceful type of power. Instead the Shaolin leopard's power is produced from loose, relaxed, whip-like techniques, which are generated by speed and balance, coupled with limber waist and hip-based movements.

To provide a balance between the solid, massive strength of a tiger and the quick, penetrating force of a crane, Shaolin monks chose the leopard as one of their five fighting animals. The Shaolin leopard form develops both physical strength and speed for the five animal practitioner. This kind of penetrating strength is called *li* by the Chinese and represents an external form of conditioning for skin, tendon, bone, and muscle.

There is little internal (qi) training available from the leopard form. Since internal development is promoted by slow, precise movements, which generate and sink the body's qi lower, the quick, sharp techniques that characterize the leopard are valuable mainly as external fighting techniques.

However, there is a definite *link* between the internal training of the dragon and snake and the leopard form's external strengths. Each one needs the other to mold together an effective fighting style.

The leopard form's primary fist is called *bao chui* (leopard fist) and is a punch designed to produce trauma with a fast, penetrating force throughout the opponent's body.

Bao chui is formed by folding the fingers forward to the first joint of the four fingers, rather than to the knuckle, as with a regular fist. The thumb is held flat along the outside of the fist, adding stability. The streamlined shape of the leopard fist has the effect of concentrating the power into a small area and increasing the overall force of the punch.

Training for bao chui involves punching firm sandbags and practicing push-ups on the knuckles instead of the hands. If the leopard form stylist's knuckles are not properly conditioned, attempts to administer bao chui blows could break his knuckles.

Not only must he have strong knuckles to produce an effective leopard fist, but his hands must also be conditioned to withstand the force behind a properly delivered bao chui. To accomplish that goal, the Shaolin leopard stylist should hold a rubber ball with both hands and squeeze with all of his strength, over 100 times each day.

The leopard form of Shaolin five animals also utilizes a regular closed fist for some techniques and several forearm and elbow strikes. The leopard is an expert at transferring his external *jing* (*ging* or power) to the area of his body that makes contact with his opponent. In the case of a bao chui, jing comes out through the knuckles. With forearm and elbow strikes, jing is released again, only at the point of contact, producing powerful, penetrating force.

One illustration that the Shaolin leopard style is an advanced form of fighting is that there are few blocking or defensive movements. Rather than block first and counterstrike, the leopard stylist will merely deflect an oncoming blow with his forearm, as his own punch simultaneously drives in. As he deflects the opposition's strike, he changes the angle of his own punch slightly to find and attack the opponent's weak area.

Footwork for the leopard form involves quick, short stances designed to stabilize and produce strong, balanced stances that can change quickly and easily from one position to another.

There are several techniques within the five animal form that characterize the leopard. *Hei bao shang shu* (black panther climbs the tree) shows the speed and aggressiveness of the leopard's attack. This technique is a rapid-fire series of four leopard fist punches delivered to both the face and torso before he can react against the leopard practitioner's attack.

Jin bao xi qiu (leopard plays ball) is a combination of leopard hand techniques and footwork. The fist is a regular closed fist, called *stamping fist*, that strikes down upon the opponent's head like a bouncing ball. At the same time that he strikes with his stamping fist, the leopard practitioner delivers a low cross-kick to the opposition's groin.

Another leopard technique is named *bao zi ding shen* (leopard steadies his body). This technique can be either a defensive or offensive action. When used as a defensive technique, it is a solid double upward block performed, in the form, from a square horse stance. On the offensive side, bao zi ding shen becomes a double fist attack to the enemy's temple.

Leopard spirit is similar to that of the tiger. The leopard student should be aggressive and fierce. The difference is that speed is of essence in the leopard form, both in technique and spirit.

Overall, the leopard form increases the speed of the five animal practitioner's strikes and footwork, plus strengthens his stances while still providing him with tremendous power and force.

Chapter Seven

Shaolin Five Animal Training Stages

There are three stages of training for the Shaolin five animal student. Each stage is considered to be equally as important as the others.

First Stage

After he has memorized the sequence of movements in the form, the student begins the first stage of training. At the first stage of five animal training, the martial artist practices the form slowly, with soft, flowing movements, as if it were a tai ji quan form.

In this manner, the five animal practitioner learns to relax and practice the set as a form of moving meditation. He uses this stage of five animal training to develop the essence of those animals that contribute internal strengths. *Shen* (spirit), the internal ability to focus intent and direct *qi* at will into all parts of the body, comes from the dragon form and is developed at this stage.

The snake contributes qi itself, which must be learned and developed through the slow movements of this first stage of training. For qi development to benefit, the martial artist's internal strength and subsequently his actual external force, qi, must be lowered as far as possible into the dan tian area of the body.

This is done through relaxation, calm, slow breathing, and a combining of the martial artist's shen (spirit) along with his complete concentration on his movements and the imaginary target beyond his hands.

Although the crane form is sometimes more lively than either the dragon or snake, it is still considered a form of internal training. The first stage of five animal training gives the student the elements of concentration and relaxation that he needs, to derive *jing* (libido) from the crane.

Besides teaching the five animal stylist the internal essences of each animal, the slow, smooth relaxation of the first stage of training provides another important benefit — health and longevity.

When the student practices the form in a slow, relaxed manner, he promotes better circulation and conditions his internal organs through proper breathing.

The correct way to breathe is natural and relaxed. However, the five animal practitioner learns to breathe slowly and from deep within his abdomen, rather than the shallow thoracic breathing seen in many untrained individuals. As he learns to breathe deeper and slower, he will also be lowering his qi and improving his circulatory system. Chinese doctors and philosophers believe this to be one of the secrets to a long, healthy life.

Second Stage

The next stage of Shaolin five animal training is practiced on the external level. In this stage, the five animal student practices the form at the speed of most kung-fu sets, while placing the emphasis on the development of external strengths and conditioning. Now is the time to develop and practice speed and power. From the tiger, he begins strengthening his bones(*gu*). The leopard becomes an important animal at this stage for his contribution of speed and strength (*li*).

At this second stage of five animal training, the student toughens and conditions his bones, tendons, and muscles. His body gains extra stamina and strength. His stances become solid foundations from which to deliver blows with speed and power.

A background in martial art basics is helpful to the student who practices the second stage of five animal training, since he needs to know how to emit his maximum external force in the most efficient way possible.

Third Stage

In the third and last stage of training for the Shaolin five animal martial practice, the student puts everything together to perform the five animal form complete with each animal's spirit and strengths. His form then becomes a balanced mixture of hard and soft techniques, comprising both external and internal movements.

He practices the snake and crane with soft smoothness and relaxation, emitting sharp power only at the moment of contact with the opponent. Intermingled with the soft, flowing movements of the snake and crane are the powerful, fast, external actions of the tiger and leopard. The dragon becomes a combination of movements, some soft and some hard, and all comprised of the dragon's spirit.

At this stage, the Shaolin five animal set is seen in its balanced complete form. Should the five animal practitioner need an internal penetrating power, it's there for him to draw upon. When he requires fast external strength, his five animal training gives it to him.

動物形象

Chapter Eight

The Shaolin Five Animal Form: *(Wu Xing Quan)*

The Shaolin five animal form is a rare set that was handed down to choy li fut Great Grandmaster Lau Bun (1894-1967) by his teacher's wife. Although it is a Shaolin martial art form, not choy li fut, it is a set that has been adopted by choy li fut masters who were once students of Lau Bun and who realize the value of internal-external training, such as that provided by this form.

Lau Bun was a famous choy li fut master, who was born in Tai Shan, Guangdong, China. He immigrated to San Francisco, California, and became well known throughout North America.

Lau Bun learned choy li fut from master Yuen Hai, who was himself of the third generation in choy li fut lineage. Yuen Hai's wife was a master of Shaolin kung-fu. She chose Lau Bun to be the only person to learn from her and teach the valuable and original Shaolin five animal form.

Lau Bun realized the true value of the five animal form when he met Yuen Hai's only son, his wife's stepson. The young man was a permanent cripple, with the left foot twisted grotesquely to one side.

He asked Yuen Hai how the injury had occurred. Yuen Hai related that, one day, his son and wife quarreled, with the result that the angry son threw a front kick at his stepmother. She grabbed his foot with a dragon technique (*dragon grabs the rainbow*) from the Shaolin five animal form and twisted his foot into a permanent disablement.

From then on, Lau Bun realized the power and fighting significance available within Shaolin five animal training, a form of training not available from any other Chinese martial art style.

He in turn taught the Shaolin five animal secrets to only those who showed promise of becoming martial art masters themselves.

Crane Flies
into the Sky

1 Feet together, palms down, eyes look to the east.

2 Push off on left foot and jump straight up to the south. Your left hand is crossed under the right hand.

Crane Stretches
Left Claw

5 Pick up your left foot. Both palms are spread, right palm up and left palm down.

6 Start in same foot position. Your right hand is forward, in front of left palm.

Crane Cools His Wings

3 The right foot lands first, into left cat stance. Both palms are spread, left in front and right in back.

4 Start in left cat stance. Your right palm scoops under the left palm.

7 Left foot kicks forward. At the same time, your left palm pushes forward and right palm pulls back.

8 Squat straight down with left hand forward.

Crane Stretches His Leg to the Right

9 Come back straight up with hands in same position.

10 Pull your left foot back to a bent position and face south. Your right hand scoops under left hand.

Crane Stretches His Leg Forward

13 Side kick with your left foot to the north. At the same time, your palms stretch forward to the south, right palm in front.

14 Pull your left foot back and, with body facing east, bring both palms together. Flip your hands backward to strike behind with the back of both palms.

Crane Stretches His Leg to the Left

11 Pivot to the south. Your left leg and right hand stretch forward to the south at the same time, left palm behind.

12 Pull your left foot back. Your right hand drops behind to meet the left hand, and both palms sweep to right. The left knee twists north.

15 The footwork is the same. Bring your palms forward and together.

16 Lean back and kick straight out. Open palms to the side with palms facing up.

Lazy Tiger Stretches
His Back Leg

17 Bring your left leg back to a folded position. Bring palms forward and together.

18 Flip palms back and bend forward.

Crane Guards
the Cave

21 Rapidly twist your hip to the left, kicking first low with the left foot, then following with a higher right kick, all in one motion. Change direction to face west. Your left palm strikes the right foot.

22 Land with the right foot crossed horizontally to the south. The right hand scoops under and up into a crane beak. The left hand guards at the elbow.

Crane Leaps Up
and Kicks Behind

19 Your left leg kicks straight back. At the same time, the fingers of both palms are thrust forward.

20 Your left foot kicks forward and up. Your right hand swings across to slap the top of the foot.

Crane Guards
His Nest

23 Your left foot crosses right to the north. The left hand scoops under and up to a crane beak. The right hand guards at the elbow.

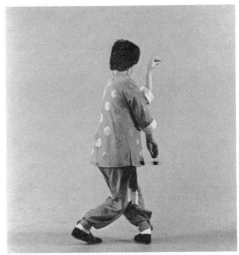

24 Take the same foot position as in #23. Your left crane beak changes to a circular block to the right.

25 Start in the same foot position. The right palm changes to a crane beak and blocks to the left.

26 Execute a right outside crescent kick to the west. The left palm slaps to the side of foot.

Crane Opens His Wings and Kicks

29 The left foot steps forward to the east in a cat stance. The right hand scoops under the left hand.

30 Pick up the left foot. Spread your palms with right palm up at head level, facing south. The left palm is down to the north.

Wild Tiger
Looks Back

27 Cross the right foot over the left foot toward the east. The right hand scoops under the left hand.

28 Same footwork. Execute a right *fu jao* (tiger claw) to rear. The left hand guards the elbow.

Dragon Grabs
the Rainbow

31 Kick straight forward.

32 Start in a left cross-stance. Pull down both hands to the left, with right claw hand in front.

Snake Climbs
Over the Log

33 Your right foot steps forward to square stance. The right hand scoops under left.

34 Take the same foot position. The right hand strikes with a backfist.

Golden Dragon
Stretches His Left Claw

37 Take a right cat stance. The left hand is under the right elbow.

38 Same footwork. The left hand stretches forward into a dragon claw at face level. The right fist is behind.

Wild Tiger
Raises His Head

35 Straighten the left foot to a bow and arrow stance. Execute a left finger jab to the eyes. Your right fist is behind.

36 Take a square stance. Execute a right uppercut. The left hand protects at the elbow.

Golden Dragon
Stretches His Right Claw

39 Take a right cat stance. The right hand scoops under the left elbow. Look to the south.

40 The right foot steps south. The right hand lifts outward.

41 Same foot position. Your right dragon claw turns to the right. The left hand protects under the right elbow.

42 Same footwork. The right palm blocks to the left.

45 Take a square stance. The right hand blocks down.

46 Take a bow and arrow stance. Execute a left finger jab forward at eye level.

43 The left foot stretches to a bow and arrow stance. The left palm blocks to the right.

44 Take a square stance. Execute a right finger thrust forward to the south.

Left and Right Closing the Door

47 Return to a square stance. Execute a right finger jab forward at eye level.

48 Start in a square stance. The right hand blocks to the left, fingers pointing up. The left hand follows below the right, fingers pointing down.

49 Still in a square stance, your right hand blocks to the left. The left hand follows below.

50 Still in a square stance, the left hand blocks to the right. The right hand follows below.

Snake Comes Out of His Hole to the Left

53 From a square stance, the left hand blocks to the right.

54 From a bow and arrow stance, the right hand blocks to the left.

Water Snake Swims
to the Surface

51 From a square stance, the right hand blocks over, above the left hand.

52 From a square stance, the left hand scoops up to the north (as if holding a mirror). The right hand protects at the elbow.

55 From a square stance, the left hand blocks to the right.

56 From a square stance, the left hand presses down. The right hand gets ready to strike.

57 From a bow and arrow stance, the right hand thrusts to eye level.

58 From a square stance, the left hand thrusts to eye level.

Snake Climbs Over a Log

61 Same footwork. Both hands pull down to the left, the right claw hand in front.

62 Your right foot steps forward to the north. Execute a right backfist.

Dragon Grabs the Rainbow

59 From a left cat stance, both palms draw back to the right.

60 Twist your left foot. Both hands stretch up in a circle.

63 From a bow and arrow stance, execute a left finger thrust forward. Your right fist is behind.

64 Start in a square stance. With a right dragon claw, grab the ribs.

Snake Comes Out
of His Hole

65 From a bow and arrow stance, your left hand thrusts forward.

66 From a square stance, your right hand thrusts forward.

69 Your left foot retreats to the east. Your right hand is ready to strike.

70 From a bow and arrow stance, your right dragon claw swings horizontally west to your opponent's face.

Golden Dragon
Tests His Claws

67 From a square stance, your right hand blocks to the left.

68 From a bow and arrow stance, your left hand blocks to the right.

Black Panther
Climbs the Tree

71 Straighten your left leg. Drop both hands down and to the right.

72 Your left foot steps forward to the north into a square stance. Your palms circle up. Your left hand is in front.

73 Turn to a bow and arrow stance, and throw a right leopard fist to the face. Your left fist protects at your chest.

74 From a square stance, throw a left leopard fist to the ribs. Your right fist protects at your chest.

Dragon Stretches His Right Claw

77 From a square stance, your right hand scoops under the left elbow. Face east.

78 Your right foot steps east into a square stance. Your right hand scoops up into a dragon claw.

75 From a bow and arrow stance, throw a right leopard fist to the ribs. Your left fist protects at the chest.

76 From a square stance, throw a left leopard fist to the face. Your right fist protects at the chest.

Dragon Swings His Claw

79 From a square stance, your right hand blocks to the left.

80 From a bow and arrow stance, your left hand blocks to the right. Look north.

Snake Climbs
Over a Log

81 Your right foot retreats to the south. Your right claw swings horizontally to the north and strikes at the ribs. Your left hand is behind.

82 Turn around and face south in a square stance.

Leopard Rolls
the Ball

85 Take a horizontal bow and arrow stance, with the left leg straight, facing east. Your left hand circles to block across the chest and then straight down.

86 Your right knee bends toward the floor. Your right fist blocks across horizontally. Your left palm protects at the right elbow.

83 From a square stance, throw a right backfist.

84 From a bow and arrow stance, with the left leg straight, throw a left finger jab forward to the south at eye level.

Dragon Stretches
His Left Claw

87 Your right foot shifts to the south to a square stance. Execute a right reverse hammerfist to the groin. Your left hand protects at the chest.

88 Your left foot steps a half-step forward up to the right foot. Your left hand crosses under the right elbow.

Wild Tiger
Raises His Head

89 Take a right cat stance. Your dragon claw stretches out. Your right hand protects the side of the head.

90 Your right foot steps forward to a square stance to the south. Your right hand scoops forward.

Golden Dragon
Thrusts His Right Claw

93 From a bow and arrow stance, execute a left finger thrust to eye level.

94 From a square stance, your right dragon claw grabs the ribs.

Snake Climbs
Over a Log

91 From a square stance, execute a right eyebrow-level uppercut. Your left hand protects at the elbow.

92 From a square stance, drop your right fist down.

Snake Comes Out
of His Hole

95 From a bow and arrow stance, execute a left finger thrust to eye level.

96 From a square stance, execute a right finger thrust forward, over the top of the left hand.

Dragon Stretches
His Left Leg

97 Take a bow and arrow stance, facing east. Both hands draw down to the right.

98 Throw a left kick to the east, at stomach level.

Crane Opens
Left Wing

101 Your right foot pivots to the right. Your right fist blocks down.

102 Your left foot steps forward to the east in a square stance. Your left hand cuts across horizontally, palm facing down. The right palm is up, next to the elbow.

Dragon Stretches
His Right Leg

99 Your left foot crosses in front of your right foot. Both hands pull down to the left. Throw a right kick to the front, at stomach level.

Leopard Twists
His Neck

100 Your right foot steps forward to a square stance. Your right hand circles to a backfist; your left hand protects at the shoulder.

Crane Strikes
with His Wing

103 From a square stance, the left hand blocks to right, the right hand is behind the hip.

104 From a square stance, your right hand blocks to the left (facing south). Your left hand is behind you.

Dragon Thrusts
His Right Claw

105 The left foot retreats to the north to a bow and arrow stance. Your left hand cuts across horizontally from left to right at eye level.

106 From a square stance, facing south, execute a right dragon claw hand to the ribs. Your left hand is at the shoulder.

109 Your right foot steps back to the north in cross-stance. Both hands reach out for a grab.

110 Turn to the right to a square stance. Move both arms toward the front, with the left hand leading.

Snake Comes Out
of His Hole

107 From a bow and arrow stance,
your left finger pokes out.

Dragon Sinks
into the Ocean

108 From a square stance, your right
finger pokes to eye level.

111 From a slant stance, both hands
pull back.

Dragon Looks
at the Sun

112 Assume a square stance. Your left
hand is ready to block up; your right fist
is behind.

Crane Strikes
with Both Wings

113 Move into a bow and arrow stance. Your left hand blocks up. Your right fist delivers an uppercut forward.

114 From a square stance, your left hand forms a cross over the right hand. Then both hands spread apart.

Dragon Sinks
into the Ocean

117 Your right foot steps forward to the west in a bow and arrow stance. Your left hand swings horizontally at eye level to the right.

118 From a square stance, both hands reach forward, with your right hand in front.

Crane Strikes
with His Left Wing

115 From a square stance, your left hand blocks to the right.

116 From a bow and arrow stance, facing west, your right hand blocks to left.

Dragon Looks
at the Sun

119 From a right slant stance, both hands pull back.

120 From a bow and arrow stance, your right palm blocks up. Execute a left uppercut forward.

Crane Strikes
with Both Wings

Crane Strikes
with His Right Wing

121 Assume a square stance. Your right hand forms a cross over the left hand. Then both hands spread apart.

122 From a square stance, your right hand blocks to the left.

Wild Tiger Pushes
the Mountain

125 Your left foot steps back to a cross-stance. Your right hand grabs, while your left hand is placed next to the left ear.

126 Assume a cross-stance. Execute a left tiger palm thrust straight forward, with fingers pointing to the right. Your right tiger claw protects the head.

123 From a bow and arrow stance, your left hand blocks to the right. Look to the south.

124 Your right foot retreats to the north to a bow and arrow stance. Your right hand swings horizontally at eye level to the left. Face the south.

Tiger Nods His Head

127 Turn to a square stance. Your left hand (tiger claw) grabs. Your right fist is forward.

128 Assume a right slant stance. Your right fist presses down. Your left claw hand is under your elbow.

Snake Climbs
Over a Log

129 Shift forward to a square stance. Your right backfist is ready to strike. Your left hand is behind.

130 Assume a bow and arrow stance with your right backfist all the way to the rear. Execute a left finger jab to the eye level.

Crane Guards
the Cave

Crane Guards
His Nest

133 Your left foot crosses the right as you face west. Your right hand scoops under and up to a crane beak. Your right hand guards at the elbow.

134 Same foot position. Form a right crane beak for a circular block to the right.

Crane Lifts
His Left Foot

131 Your left foot kicks forward and up. Your right hand swings across in front to slap the top of your foot.

Crane Stands
on One Leg

132 Turn to the left 180 degrees, facing north. Stand on your right leg, left leg up. Execute a right crane beak to the right side of the face. Your left hand protects under the right elbow.

135 Same foot position. The left palm blocks to the left.

136 Execute a right outside crescent kick to the west. The left palm slaps to the side of your foot.

Dragon Grabs
the Rainbow

137 Your right foot steps to the south. Turn to face the north.

138 From a left cat stance, facing north, your left palm blocks down. Your right palm protects the elbow.

Dragon Stretches
His Right Leg

141 From a square stance, execute a left finger jab at eye level. Your right palm is near your left elbow.

142 Your left foot twists north. Both hands are ready to grab.

139 Your left foot steps out to square stance. Your right hand pulls over, and your left dragon claw presses down.

140 From a bow and arrow stance, execute a right finger jab to eye level.

143 Assume a cross-stance, left foot forward. Both dragon claw hands pull down to the left.

144 Your right foot kicks forward to the north. Both hands pull to the south.

Wild Tiger
Looks Back

145 Cross your right foot over the left, toward the south. Your right hand scoops under the left hand to form a right tiger claw to the north. Your left hand guards at the elbow.

Crane Spreads
His Wings

146 Turn to the left, facing east. Your right hand scoops under the left hand.

Leopard Twists
His Body

149 Your right foot steps forward to a square stance. Your right hand pulls across and your left dragon claw presses down.

150 From a square stance, your left hand blocks to the right. Your right hand forms a fist next to the right ear.

Dragon Grabs
the Rainbow

147 Assume a cat stance, with your right palm up and next to the head. Your left palm blocks down.

148 Assume a cat stance, with both palms to the left side.

Crane Opens
His Right Wing

151 Your left foot twists while your right forearm blocks horizontally.

152 Your right foot steps east to a square stance. Your right hand cuts across horizontally to the right, with palm facing downward at shoulder level. Your left palm faces up, next to the elbow.

Snake Comes Out
of His Hole

153 From a bow and arrow stance, execute a left finger jab at eye level.

154 From a square stance, execute a right finger jab at eye level. Your left palm protects your elbow.

Black Dragon Swings
His Tail

157 Your right foot steps forward to the southwest. Your right dragon claw turns to the right. Your left hand protects under the right elbow.

158 From a square stance, your right hand blocks in front of your face. Your left hand is under your elbow.

Dragon Looks Back

Golden Dragon
Stretches His Right Claw

155 Turn to the west in a slant stance. You left palm strike to the groin level, with your palm facing up. Your right hand protects your head.

156 Your left foot twists, while your right hand lifts outward. Face southwest.

Golden Dragon Stretches
His Right Claw

159 Your left foot steps back to the southwest into a cross-stance. Both hands split apart in opposite directions.

160 Turn to a left slant stance. Your left hand blocks down.

161 Twist your left foot. Your right claw hand scoops under.

162 Your right foot steps forward to the southwest in a square stance. Your right dragon claw turns to the right. The left hand protects under the right elbow.

Golden Dragon Stretches His Right Claw

165 Turn to a left slant stance. Your left hand blocks down.

166 Twist your left foot. Your right claw hand scoops under.

Black Dragon Swings
His Tail

163 Your right foot steps back to a cross-stance. Your right palm crosses horizontally in front of your face. The left hand is under the elbow.

164 Same foot position. Face southwest. Your hands split apart in opposite directions.

167 Your right foot steps forward to the southwest into a square stance. Your right dragon claw turns to the right. Your left hand protects under the right elbow.

168 Assume a diagonal bow and arrow stance and face east. Your right hand blocks across the left hand.

Green Dragon Comes Up
from the Ocean to the Right

169 Your left leg retreats to the north in a horizontal bow and arrow stance. Your left finger pokes forward at eye level to the east. Your right hand protects at the elbow.

170 Take a horizontal bow and arrow stance. Your left hand circles and blocks down. Your right fist is on your hip.

Leopard Plays Ball
to the Right

173 From a kneeling stance, left knee down, your left fist punches forward. Your right hand protects the head.

174 Same position. Your left hand circles and blocks down. Your right fist is behind.

171 From a kneeling stance, with your right knee down, your right fist punches forward. Your left hand protects the head.

172 Same position. Your right hand circles and blocks down. Your left fist is on your hip.

175 From a kneeling stance, right knee down, your right fist blocks across horizontally. Your left palm protects at the elbow.

176 From a bow and arrow stance, your right fist blocks down. Your left fist is ready to strike.

177 Execute a right crescent kick to the left. At the same time, your left fist swings down to the right. Your right hand is behind.

178 From a bow and arrow stance, your right fist swings to the left in a downward strike. Your left fist is behind.

181 Launch a left crescent kick to the right. Your right fist strikes down to the left. Your left fist is behind.

182 Your left foot steps back to the northwest into a diagonal bow and arrow stance. Your left fist swings to the right in a downward strike. Your right fist is behind.

Leopard Plays Ball to the Left

179 Assume a kneeling position, left knee down. Your left fist blocks across horizontally. Your right palm protects at the elbow.

180 From a bow and arrow stance, your left fist blocks down. Your right fist is behind.

Leopard Looks at the Moon

Snake Climbs Over a Log

183 Take a right slant stance. Your right fist swings down. Your left palm protects your head.

184 Your right foot moves back one-half step to a cat stance. Your right backfist is down. Your left palm is at the shoulder, fingers forward.

Leopard Scratches
His Back

185 Same position. Your left finger jabs at eye level. Your right fist is behind.

186 From a square stance, your right elbow swings horizontally to the left. Your right palm strikes the elbow.

Snake Looks
at the Road

189 Shift forward to a right square stance. Execute a right uppercut with the elbow. Your left palm protects at the chest.

190 From a bow and arrow stance, your left finger jabs at eye level. Your right fist is behind.

187 Same position. Your left palm scoops up, inside the right elbow.

188 From a square stance, execute a right horizontal elbow strike to the south. Your left palm pushes out to the north.

Green Dragon Comes Up from the Sea

191 From a square stance, execute a right punch straight to the ribs. Your left hand protects at the elbow.

Twin Cranes Raise Their Heads

192 Your right leg crosses to the west. Your right hand scoops across and under the left hand. Face east.

White Snake Throws Out His Tongue

193 Same position. Both hands, in crane beak position, stretch out to east and west.

194 Turn to the left into a square stance, facing east. Your left hand blocks down. Your right snake tongue is positioned next to the right ear.

197 Take a bow and arrow stance. Your left tiger claw is forward at face level. Your right claw is next to the right knee. Face southeast.

198 Your left foot steps forward to the northeast into a square stance. Your left hand blocks down. Your right tiger claw is next to the right ear.

Hungry Tiger Catches the Lamb

195 From a bow and arrow stance, a right snake tongue pokes forward at eye level. Your left hand is behind.

196 Your right foot steps forward to the southeast into a square stance. Your right hand blocks down. Your left tiger claw hand is next to the left ear.

199 From a bow and arrow stance, bring your right tiger claw forward to face level. Your left claw hand is next to the left knee.

200 Your right foot steps forward to the southeast into a square stance. Your right hand blocks down. Your left tiger claw is next to the ear.

201 From a bow and arrow stance, bring your left tiger claw forward to face level. Your right claw hand is next to the knee.

202 Your left foot steps forward to the northeast to a square stance. Your left hand blocks down. Your right claw hand is next to the right ear.

Green Dragon Comes Up from the Ocean

205 From a bow and arrow stance, bring your left claw hand forward to face level. Your right claw hand is next to the knee.

206 From a bow and arrow stance, your left hand circles down to block. Your right fist is at the waist.

203 From a bow and arrow stance, bring your right tiger claw forward to the face level. Your left claw hand is next to the knee.

204 Your right foot steps forward to the southeast. Your right hand blocks down. Your left tiger claw is next to the left ear.

207 Your right foot retreats to the south. Execute a right punch straight to the chest. Your left hand protects at the elbow.

208 Same position. Your right hand circles and blocks down. Your left fist is ready to punch.

209 Your left foot retreats to the northwest. Your left fist punches to the chest level. Your right fist protects at the elbow.

210 Assume a bow and arrow stance. Your left hand circles down to block, while your right fist is on your waist.

Left and Right
Closing the Door

213 Your left foot retreats to the northwest. Your left fist punches straight to the chest. Your right fist protects at the elbow.

214 Take a diagonal square stance. Your right palm blocks to the left, with your fingers pointing up. Your left hand blocks down to the left, fingers pointing down.

211 Your right foot retreats to the southwest. Execute a right punch straight to the chest. Your left hand protects at the elbow.

212 Same position. Your right hand circles and blocks down. Your left fist is ready to punch.

215 Same position. Your right hand blocks down. Your left hand is turned upward, ready to block.

216 Take a square stance. Your left hand blocks across to the right, fingers up. Your right hand blocks down to the left.

Wild Tiger
Looks Back

217 Take a square stance. Your right hand scoops under to the left. Your left hand is next to the shoulder.

218 Your right foot crosses to the west. Execute a right tiger claw to the east. Your left hand protects at the elbow. Face east.

Snake Chases a Stick

221 Your left foot closes to the right, as you bend your knees. Execute a right backfist downward. Your left palm is at the right shoulder.

222 Your right foot kicks forward. Your left finger jabs at eye level.

Leopard Stamps
the Ground

219 Turn to the west. Your left hand circles and blocks down. Your right fist is at the back.

220 Take a square stance. Your right fist swings down vertically to knee level. Your left hand blocks across the chest.

Green Dragon Comes Up
from the Ocean

223 Your right foot steps to square stance. Execute a right punch to the west. Your left palm protects at the right elbow.

Poison Snake Blocks
the Road

224 Assume a square stance. Your right hand blocks to the left. Your left hand is ready to strike.

225 Your left foot steps forward to the southwest into a square stance. Your left palm chops across horizontally to the southwest at shoulder level, fingers level. Your right palm faces up at chest level.

226 Face northwest in a square stance. Your left palm blocks to the right. Your right palm is ready to strike.

229 Your left foot steps forward to the southwest in a square stance. Your left palm chops across horizontally to the southwest at shoulder level, fingers level. Your right palm is up and at chest level.

230 Face northwest in a square stance. Your left palm blocks to the right. Your right palm is ready to chop.

227 Your right foot steps to the northwest. Your right palm chops across horizontally to the right. Your left hand is up at chest level.

228 Assume a square stance, facing southwest. Your right hand blocks down to the left. Your left hand is ready to chop.

Left and Right
Closing the Door

231 Your right foot steps to the northwest. Your right palm chops across horizontally to the right. Your left palm is up at chest level.

232 Take a diagonal square stance. Your right hand blocks to the left, fingers pointing up. Your left palm blocks down to the left, fingers pointing downward. Face southwest.

233 Same position. Your right hand blocks down. Your left hand is turned upward, ready to block.

234 Same position. Your left hand blocks across to the right, fingers pointing up. Your right hand blocks down to the right, fingers pointing down.

Leopard Steadies His Body

237 Assume a cross-stance. Execute a right tiger claw to the west. Your left hand protects at the right elbow.

238 Turn to the east and jump up. Both hands stretch upward.

Wild Tiger
Looks Back

235 Take a diagonal square stance. Pull back both hands, with the right hand in front. Look to the west.

236 Your right foot crosses to the east. Your right hand scoops under to the left. Your left hand is next to the shoulder.

Bowing to Buddha
in Lotus Position

239 Land in a front square stance, facing east. Both fists are above your head, facing one another.

240 Take a square stance. The back of both palms strike backward.

241 Cross both legs, right foot in front. Both palms come back to shoulder level.

242 Both knees on the floor and spread outward. Both palms are together.

245 Rapidly twist your hip to the left, kicking, first low with the left foot, then following with a higher kick, all in one motion. Change direction to face west.

246 Your left palm strikes the right foot in midair. Land on the left foot.

Crane Leaps Up and Kicks Behind

243 Get up on the right leg, left foot ready to kick. Your right palm is ready to strike down. Your left hand is next to your body.

244 Your left foot kicks forward and up. Your right hand swings across to slap the top of the foot.

Green Dragon Comes Up from the Ocean

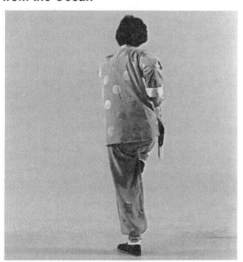

247 Stand on the left leg and raise your right knee. Your left palm blocks down. Your right fist is next to your waist. Face west.

248 Your right foot steps forward into a square stance. Execute a right punch straight forward. Your left palm blocks across the chest.

Sit Back and Ride
the Tiger

249 Turn to the east in a bow and arrow stance. Your right hand blocks down. Your left hand is behind.

250 Assume a cat stance, left foot forward. Your left palm blocks across the body and stops at the right hip. Your right hand protects the head.

Twin Snakes Look
Over the Log

253 Same foot position. Both palms flip back.

254 Same foot position. Both hands come up above shoulders, palms facing forward.

Crane Cools
His Wings

251 Take a left cat stance. Your right palm scoops under the left palm.

252 Pick up the left foot. Both palms are spread, right palm up and left palm down.

Conclusion

255 Your left foot kicks forward to the east. At the same time, both hands, fingers forward, poke to the east.

256 Your left foot comes down to cat stance. Both palms flip backward.

257 Same position. Put your right fist and left palm together to salute the east.

258 Turn your body south, with both hands open forward, palms exposed.

261 Your right foot steps back to close with the left. Both fists pull back to the waist. Face south.

262 Attention position. Both palms push down toward floor.

259 Same position. Both hands make fists and pull back to the chest.

260 Your left foot steps back to the north. Both fists roll downward in a backfist position.

五形之手法運用

Chapter Nine

Application of Shaolin Five Animal Techniques

Golden Dragon Tests His Claws

1 Opponent punches to Wong's face.

2 Wong blocks down with his right hand to the attacker's punching hand with a circular block called *poon kiu*.

5 Wong's right hand forms a dragon claw.

6 Wong steps forward with his right foot to trip his attacker, while his dragon claw hand smashes into the opponent's face.

3 Opponent counters with a right punch to Wong's face.

4 Wong's left hand blocks opponent's punch with a poon kiu and at the same time traps the opposition's other hand.

Dragon Tests
His Right Claw

1 Opponent throws a right punch to Wong's face.

2 Wong's right hand blocks and traps the attacker's punching arm.

3 Wong's left hand forms a dragon claw and grabs the attacker's ribs with a squeezing motion.

4 At the same time, Wong's right hand grabs the opponent's throat with a dragon claw hand.

Wild Tiger
Looks Back

1 Opponent punches to Wong's chest.

2 Wong blocks with an inward right forearm.

3 Wong's left leg retreats to a *stealing* stance and his left hand grabs the opponent's wrist.

4 Wong's right hand delivers a tiger claw hand to his attacker's face.

Hungry Tiger
Captures a Lamb

1 Opponent delivers a right kick to Wong's stomach. Wong's left hand scoops under his attacker's leg to stop and block the oncoming kick.

2 Wong's attacker steps forward and punches with a left fist to Wong's face.

3 Wong's left hand blocks the punch with a downward slap.

4 Wong grabs his opponent's left hand and, at the same time, administers a right tiger claw to the attacker's face.

1 Opponent grabs Wong's right hand.

2 Attacker punches at Wong's face with a right fist.

3 Wong lifts and twists his right arm to bring pressure against the attacker's thumb and break his grab. At the same time, Wong lifts his right arm up to block the oncoming punch.

4 Wong rolls the attacker's right arm over the top of his left arm and then pins it with his own right hand.

Continued

5 Wong administers a left snake finger strike to the opponent's throat.

White Snake Throws Out His Tongue

1 Opponent grabs Wong's left hand.

2 Opponent punches to Wong's left rib.

3 Wong twists his grabbed hand free and blocks the punch.

4 Wong rolls his opponent's right hand over the left and traps his opponent's hands.

Continued

117

5 While controlling the attacker, Wong delivers a right snake finger strike to his opponent's throat.

1 Opponent throws a left punch to Wong's chest.

2 Wong blocks with a right inward block.

3 Opponent then punches with the right fist to Wong's face.

4 Wong uses a right crane neck fist to block the punch.

Continued

5 Opponent counters with a left fist to Wong's ribs. Wong drops his right crane neck down to block the oncoming punch.

6 Wong hooks both of his opponent's arms with his right crane neck, and proceeds to strike into his attacker's eyes with a left crane beak.

Crane Strikes
with His Wings

1 Opponent throws a right kick to Wong's stomach. Wong's left hand blocks down.

2 Opponent punches with left fist to Wong's face.

3 Wong blocks down.

4 Wong counters with a right horizontal fingertip strike, aimed at the opponent's eyes.

Continued

5 Wong makes contact with the opponent's eye with his crane wing strike.

6 Wong cuts through with the crane wing strike.

1 Opponent punches to Wong's face with a right punch.

2 Wong blocks up with his right hand.

3 Wong pulls down and holds opponent's right hand while delivering left leopard fist to face.

4 Wong lets go of opponent's right hand and punches straight into opposition's solar plexus with a right leopard fist, while shifting one-half step forward.

Continued

5 At the same time, Wong administers a left leopard fist to opposition's neck.

Leopard Plays Ball

1 Opponent punches to Wong's face with left punch.

2 Wong blocks across with right arm.

3 Opponent counters with a right punch to Wong's face.

4 Wong's left leopard fist also blocks opponent's right punch. At the same time, Wong kicks his opponent's ribs.

Continued

125

5 After his kick, Wong's left fist comes straight down, still controlling opponent's right arm.

6 Wong uses his waist to deliver a right leopard fist to opponent's head, like a bouncing ball.

About the Authors

DOC-FAI WONG

Doc-Fai Wong, a member of the fifth generation in choy li fut lineage, is one of the highest-ranking practitioners in the United States. He has had over 20 years in training in choy li fut kung-fu.

Born in Kwangtung, China in 1948, Wong came to the United States via Macao at age 11. Always interested in martial arts, Doc-Fai Wong got his chance to learn in San Francisco when he discovered *tai ji quan* (tai chi chuan) and Shaolin martial arts instructors in Chinatown. He learned Shaolin from Kuo Poi Liu and tai ji quan from L. G. Fok.

At age 14, Wong was accepted as a disciple by choy li fut grandmaster Lau Bun. The same year he became a disciple of Chan (Zen) master, Hsuan Hua, the abbot of the City of Ten Thousand Buddhas.

He studied from Lau Bun until his master's death in 1967. At that time, Wong assisted Lau Bun's successor, Lang Jew, for two years in the San Francisco school.

In 1969, encouraged to start his own school by Jew, Wong became one of the first traditional kung-fu teachers to venture outside San Francisco's Chinatown with his martial arts school. He was also one of the first to include non-Chinese students in his teaching regimen.

Although he studied and teaches choy li fut, Wong made the Shaolin five animal form one of his favorite sets. He realized the benefits and improvement over any other martial arts animal forms when five animal spirit and techniques were correctly practiced. As a result, Doc-Fai Wong became Lau Bun's primary Shaolin five animal form demonstrator, and soon gained the nickname throughout San Francisco's Chinatown in the late 1960s as the "Five Animal Kid."

Nowadays, Doc-Fai Wong has put all his training together to further the promotion of Chinese martial arts. He is the president of the Choy Li Fut International Federation with over 40 branch schools in the United States and Europe.

He is an instructor of tai ji quan, having learned from and become a disciple of Woo Van-Cheuk (himself a student of Yang Cheng Fu, the grandson and best-known promoter of Yang style tai ji). Besides teaching in his own school, Wong teaches the largest tai ji quan class in the San Francisco Bay area on a daily basis for the San Francisco Community College.

He also is a California State Certified Acupuncturist and Doctor of Oriental medicine.

Besides this book, Wong is the author of *Choy Li Fut Kung Fu* (Unique Publications).

JANE HALLANDER

Jane Hallander has been writing martial arts articles for magazines, both in the United States and abroad, since 1980. She has written well over 200 articles covering a wide range of styles.

Hallander is a long-time student of Chinese martial arts. She teaches a tai ji quan class in San Francisco, besides practicing choy li fut kung-fu. She knows the Shaolin five animal form and uses its principles throughout her tai ji quan and external kung-fu practice. She also is a student and practitioner of qi qong.

Hallander is the author of *Guide to Kung Fu Fighting Styles*, and the co-author of *Choy Li Fut Kung Fu* and *Korea's Fighting Weapons*.